Seasons
By
Kennedy Scott

ISBN: 9798218498894 (Paperback)

Cover Design: Kennedy Scott
First Printing Edition: 2024

Dedications:

To My Mama: Thank you for your continuation of support and love in my life. You are a huge reason I wake up and aspire to be a better person each and every day. I hope I continue to make you proud.

To Granny Nora: You continue to be the purest example of love. You will always hold a giant place in my heart. Thank you for never failing to encourage me to be the most authentic version of myself.

To the Merp and Zee: Thank you both for continuing to be such a beautiful addition to my days. Your encouragement, understanding, and acceptance means the world to me. I'm so happy to call you both not only friends, but like a little family to me. I can not imagine my days without both of your guys' brightness in it.

To Erin: Thank you for being the brightest, most genuine sense of summer I've ever experienced. I feel so lucky to be able to tackle life by your side, and I can't wait to keep growing with you as the seasons change. Thank you so much for being my 7 minutes. I love you.

Authors Note:

I began writing *Seasons* before *Almosts* was officially released. I wanted to be able to finish the chapter of longing and missing someone while also embracing the fact that life would continue to move forward. I have been fortunate enough to experience the hope of love, growth, and change in the time since beginning to write this collection. Throughout writing this book I have weathered some storms, lost and found feelings of hope, lost connections, fell in love and found a deeper understanding of myself.

This book dives into a more thorough sense of self-reflection, vulnerability, and self-exploration than I've ever displayed or expressed before. I am so proud of how my writing and perspective has evolved as *Seasons* has unfolded.

Thank you all for reading.

Table Of Contents:

Spring, Summer, Fall, & Winter

Spring:
Hope, Optimism, & Growth

Summer
Love, Joy, & Warmth

Fall

Mourning, Longing, & Chasing Closure

Winter

Grief, Sadness, Bitterness & Anger

An Introduction to Seasons
(From my Summer)

It is my pleasure to introduce Kennedy's second book, Seasons!

I've technically known her for a while now, as she has been a regular at my place of work for a little over a year (she has a massive coffee/rebel addiction if you didn't know). We always used to just talk in passing, but after a while, she decided to ask me out one day and I said yes - it only took her over six months but we got there eventually! She took me bowling (in which I absolutely destroyed her), and afterwards she took me to one of her favorite spots along the waterfront to see bunnies and look at the stars.

Since then I've had the pleasure of falling hopelessly in love.

Kennedy is such a unique person, she has this radiance about her that is so intriguing it makes you want to know her more. She is so inspiring with her work, so eloquent with her words, and so unbelievably brilliant. She's also loving, patient, supportive, charming, sincere, hardworking, affectionate, authentic, kind-hearted, and so much more.

When I met Kennedy, it had only been a couple
of months after her first book, Almosts, came
out and I've watched as she's poured so much
time and energy into bringing Seasons to life.

When she told me about her concept for Seasons
I was immediately hooked. Her book is overrun
with raw emotion, from hope, prosperity, and
adoration, to wistfulness, longing, dread, and
spite; Seasons encapsulates it all.

Spring is all about bringing in positive energy
and letting personal growth happen, with an
overview of hopefulness for the future; almost
like planting roots and seeing them start to bud
into something new.

Summer feels like letting in the sun and feeling
the warmth of a new love and pure bliss, it's
very bright and full of colors and imagery of
euphoria.

Fall has a sense of longing and wistfulness, it's
very somber and sort of gray and overcast.
You'll feel as though you're falling into a bit of
anxiety as the change in season happens,
uncertain where it will bring you and you'll find
yourself mourning the past.

Winter will wrap up the seasons with themes of
grief, anger, and pent-up bitterness. You'll go
through the motions of loss, regret, misery,
contempt, and ultimate catharsis.

As someone who Kennedy has branded as her
own sense of summer, I'm very excited to have
you see the passion Kennedy has put into
creating this book. I'm so unbelievably proud of
her and all she's accomplished and I can't wait
to see what the future holds, for both her, and us.
Thank you all for reading.

And to my Pookie, I love you, big, like dinosaur
<3

- E

Spring

Hope, Optimism, & Growth

Seasons

With each passing year
as I watch the seasons
come and go
I understand
much like the color of the leaves
my outlook shifts in color
allowing a different perspective

As I have made my way
through many a fall
mourning loves and lives
I thought I would want
for the rest of my existence
the deepest yearning
to hold on to the familiar
regardless of the reality
of the pain and sacrifice
so I stumble

Winter takes over
a familiarity in the darkness
a dreaded anticipation
for getting through it
because even after the brighter months
I know it will rear its bitter head
once again

Kennedy Scott

A sigh of relief in spring
the weight lifted off my shoulders
as I embrace a sense of hope
a chance to move on
the opportunity to start again
and forget all of the bitter winters
hoping for a comfortable summer
and having faith
that when fall circles back
I can admire the trees

The beauty of summer
the overtaking in growth
a chance to stop and smell the roses
appreciating beauty
turning life into a movie
falling so deep in love
with what life has to offer
I forget the other seasons
will circle back around

I am fully aware
of the cyclical nature
of the ever changing seasons
I know now
that I am in control of my perspective
the coldness of fall and winter
do not have to dictate the narrative
of the rest of my year

Kennedy Scott

I embrace the chance
to heal during fall
to make it through winter
to embrace hope during spring
and to fall in love during summer

Without fall
and the changing leaves
I would not look forward to Spring
with fresh blooms and the rays of sun
without the harshness of winter
I would not appreciate
the summer warmth
and the clearest skies
wrapped up in a sweet baby blue

Seasons are essential
for perspective and continuation
the harshest nights lead to the calmest days
and the biggest change
is being grateful for all of it
not holding regrets for things I can not control
I am grateful because I learn from it
I embrace my winters
as much as I embrace my summers
my changes in seasons
are what make me a whole person
not controlled by a single part

-K.S.

Kennedy Scott

Everest

It doesn't have to be Mt. Everest
to feel like a fight for your life
it doesn't have to be all or nothing
for it to feel like summiting new heights
because when we're at our lowest
everything feels
like a 30,000-foot summit

I'm proud of you -
regardless of your own expectations
for defying the odds
and getting out of bed

I'm proud of you -
for listening to a shred of reason,
even if from others
since your own head is clouded
with such doubt

I'm proud of you -
for allowing yourself
a sliver of hope -
even if it feels so quiet
and finding the ability
to take the first steps
to love yourself

Kennedy Scott

It's not Everest
but it is a mountainous undertaking
an endeavor into the unknown
the possibilities of a future
you've only dreamed about
a journey you've spent years pursuing
just to find out
you were working towards an alternate ending

Your own Everest
can not be conquered
without moments to
stop
breathe
and acclimate to the environment

With a few deep breaths
and one small step at a time
you'll realize
you were much better
at climbing than you thought
and as you reach the top
and you return to camp
with a different perspective
know that there are
open arms, opportunity, and love
waiting to welcome you
to your new life
                    -K.S.

Root-bound

A stunted growth -
not harmful
nor deadly
but a complete pause
in the journey of growing
reaching for the sun
and pursuing the silver lining

Risks in making moves
necessary to encourage a continuation
of heading in the right direction
and pursuing new heights
amidst the tribulations of living

A home that once set down the foundation
a chance to prove ourselves
to grow and learn
now holds us back
as our roots crowd our surroundings
we must say goodbye -
not without mourning the home
we once held near
saying goodbye to the environment
that got us here -
the position to move up
to find a new home

Kennedy Scott

I find myself root-bound
eager to find a new pot
to allow me to reach a little higher
to find a new brightness in life
and allow my roots to plant a little deeper
to get through
this newest phase of growth
-K.S.

Kennedy Scott

Love Of My Life

I've been seeking externally
a defining subject of love
to exemplify what happiness
could be
should be
what I need it to be

Determination to not fail
led me to say
there is no greater
than you and I
you're the love of my life
who else could it be?

When external sources leave
and all that's left is me
it's sink or swim
a battle to grow
or let go
and fall

The silver lining
is the void of necessity
for external sources
to prove to me
I'm somebody

Kennedy Scott

I always thought
you were the love of my life
until I recognized
it's me
the words I write
the records I spin
the desire to evolve
and give others the hope
that true love
comes from within
                    -K.S.

Looking Back

I go through periods of reflection
looking back and trying to comprehend
what's gotten me to this place
this point in my life
allowing myself
a pat on the back
for the trials and challenges
I've overcome and conquered
despite not wanting to

A celebration of strength-
often overlooked
and brushed off
because I didn't have a choice
fight or flight kicks in
with a deeper acknowledgement
that I *will* fight
to not only survive
but find a meaning in the opportunity
to allow myself to really live

I accept what I think I deserve
and through each experience in life
as I embrace reflection being 20-20
I get a little closer
to understanding that what I deserve
is far more than what I could have anticipated

Kennedy Scott

I have a sense of remorse
and a sliver of compassion
that it's taken me so long
to understand that I am capable
of embracing a future
where I am treated well
by not only the influences
I allow externally
but also treated well
by the voice I let run my person
and my motivations in life

I have embraced the steps it takes
to get a little closer
to allowing a reality
of what I soulfully
and honestly
deserve
love without limits
love without restrictions
love without conditions
                    -K.S.

Breadcrumbs

There should never be a point
where love feels like a sacrifice
of self worth
self love
self respect
and value
and yet as you left me nothing but breadcrumbs
I was convinced I could find a way
to find nourishment for a lifetime

It felt like a favor
to want to spend time with you
to want to build on a connection
I thought was mutual

It felt like a favor
to want you to love me
in the same way I loved you

I am worth more than the breadcrumbs
you try to convince yourself
is an expression of love

I am worth more than the breadcrumbs
of tiny morsels of hope
that you collect and mash together
to convince me it's romance

Kennedy Scott

As I realized I was worth more
than the tiny fragments of a whole picture
you drop behind you calling it effort
saying I should be satisfied
I was left starving for a genuine sense of love
the feeling of being cared for

Yet as I drew boundaries
all you could say was I've changed
I'm mean now
because a version of me that includes strength
self worth, and self love
is not a version of me
that will accept your breadcrumbs
and try to repackage it as love

As the seasons pass
I know I'm in for a long winter
before summer comes around
and as the environment evolves
I learn to embrace the ebbs and flows
I wouldn't appreciate the sun without the snow
and I wouldn't appreciate
the changes in the leaves
that lead to a brighter sense of green

I look forward to a brighter summer
with greater hope
than the breadcrumbs you left me
                              -K.S.

Kennedy Scott

Secure Dependance

Understanding the root
of comfort in independance
came from a place
of understanding codependence
errors in attachment that led to failed ties

Feeling without obligation
is when you find
the most security in yourself
and the least amount
of dependency in others

Freedom from unhealthy dependency
finding comfort in solitude
security in loneliness
allowed me to depend on loved ones
embracing safety
allowing loneliness
to feel allowable

Embracing love
the butterflies
and even the almosts
without a sense of obligation
in timeline, definitions, or ultimatums
allowed standards and boundaries
to exist without the feeling of guilt

Kennedy Scott

Security in dependance
security in independance
cohesive and comforting
the only relationship that *has* to exist
to find love for a lifetime

I have never felt more secure
I have never felt more independent
and I have never felt less obligation
towards the unfairly dependent environment
love can be healthy
love can be healing
love can be mine
                    -K.S.

Chasing Sunsets

I fall in love
with the falling sun
finding beauty in remoteness
the further I am
the more vibrant the display

Occasionally we need a moment
to breathe
and take in what is happening
all around us each day
to influence how we react
to various circumstances

Sometimes life does look the nicest
right before the darkness approaches
but even as it gets dark
there's beauty to be embraced
as the stars fill the sky
if we adapt to our surroundings
we see even more

I am in love with the idea
of embracing momentary glimpses
of the purest beauty
that can only appear
in moments of transition
at the end of a long day

Kennedy Scott

I am in love with the concept
that even on cloudy days
it leads to the most picturesque moments
that regardless of the nature
of how my day went
I have a beautiful display of change
to look forward to

I love chasing sunsets
because it means I made it
through another day
it helps me celebrate the moments
wrapped up in my love's arms
embracing hope and peace
and it helps me lay to rest
the days that are darker
but with each passing sunset
I embrace the fact
that I have another one to look forward to
after I welcome tomorrow
                              -K.S.

Recognition

I hold the utmost pride
knowing that my character
reflects my actions
the way I treat people
reflects my heart
and the forgiveness I pass
allows an opportunity to grow
for both parties

I wish the best
even for those who have hurt me
I hold compassion for those
who were unable to love
because I fully know
there was once a time
where I was trying to learn
myself

I celebrate each and every soul
who has embraced recognition
in the errs of their way
allowing a chance to improve
and learn from the decisions they've made
even if I have been on the receiving side
of mistakes
and maltreatment

Kennedy Scott

I am able to recognize
that the purity of my heart
leaves room for remorse
and although I will never put myself
in the position of being used
and abused once more
I hold the utmost hope that those
who were given the chance before
were able to use my pain
to recognize the suffering they inflict
is unnecessary and irreparable

I found the strength to grow
with each kick and blow
and while I recognize not all
will take advantage to find foundations to learn
in their faults and flaws
I will always offer a helping hand
even if it's just through acknowledging
the depths of hurt

I have forgiven
but I will never forget
                    -K.S.

Kennedy Scott

Sacrificial Love

Wasted time
wasted years
feeding into loves that were doomed
sacrificing myself
my own time
my own hope
in the name of hoping to accomplish
a societal vision of success in love

I refuse to sacrifice myself further for love
I refuse to accept anything less
than somebody's all
an entire heart and soul
as much as I give
as much as I love
I can not wait for my cup to empty
before I understand that they aren't made for me

I refuse to continue the trend
of sacrificing my future
for the hope of a future
with another person

I will be embraced by love
when the time is right
when the soul clicks
and when the stars align

Kennedy Scott

I am willing to give my all
to a heart that is willing to hold mine
but not at the expense
of my own well being
love shouldn't be sacrificial
it should be wrapped in support
compromise
comprehension
and adaptation

I will embrace my own future
self-love doesn't require sacrifice
and while at times
it can be rough around the edges
I know my heart
and I know how I can show up for others
so I will continue to use that energy
to show up for myself
and advocate for a brighter ending

-K.S.

Kennedy Scott

Rock Bottom

I've embraced the opportunity
since hitting rock bottom
understanding the value
in meaning behind life's circumstances
consequences to decisions
and the pain behind the reality

I value the multitudes of sobriety
absence of alcohol
clarity of the mind
understanding how I treat myself
and how I've allowed others
to define how I should be treated

I woke up
understanding the changes to be made
embracing the chance in valuing myself
my own heart
sense of character
and the intention in action

I have always been worth being loved
reflection on almosts showed me
the desperation behind wanting to be seen
wanting to be loved but always begging for it
never valuing connection past what *I* could offer
and I finally see things differently

Kennedy Scott

Loving is not without obstacles
past grazes of the skin
tones of voices
and promises broken
can dictate the response
to what is being currently presented
it takes patience and understanding
to find compassion in learning

I have never been the product
of how others have chosen to treat me
rather- the remorse and shift in their behavior
and how they treat others
is a product of the reality
of trying to turn a good heart dark

I refuse to be a lesson
I have learned enough myself
hitting rock bottom long before
the world found out
and hitting that low helped me realize
how tall the ceilings are

I don't hold regrets
because without mistakes
I would not hold myself
in the way I do today
worth something far beyond
the bottom I fell on
                    -K.S.

Kennedy Scott

What Ifs

What ifs have ruled my timelines
always filled with too much doubt
to continue to move forward
taking the risky steps
to move up in life

What if it doesn't work out?
ruled by the idea
of a prospective failure
not allowing the chance to win
to see the light of day
because I wouldn't
even let myself try

What is the worst that can happen?
focusing on the worst
didn't allow myself
to embrace the idea
that there could ever be a best

When I flipped the script
and changed the end of the question
life became more manageable
days became brighter
and the efficiency in prospering
multiplied ten fold

Kennedy Scott

What if it *does* work out?
if the crazy little idea I have
may just allow myself
to gain something
to make dreams come true
and allow myself to embrace
the win's I've always hoped for

What is the best that can happen?
because *good* is also an option
risk doesn't have to equal failure
risk can also bring reward

I allowed myself
the second half of a whole picture
I have paid the price too many times
the sunken cost fallacy
wrote my story
I can embrace reward
with the same passion
that I embraced the risk of failure

What if everything works out just fine?
                              -K.S.

Kennedy Scott

Searching

Searching does not yield solutions
like a pot of water
watching will falsify absent results
once I stopped looking
for honesty in happiness
it crossed my path

The joy in hope itself
looking forward to the little things
in moments it is the blue in the sky
the sun on my skin
or the feeling I get when she looks at me

I quit searching with a sense of necessity
and embraced circumstance
coincidence
and the flow of chance
to find an abundance of beauty
in the mornings I embrace
as I wake up and find hope
in each and every little moment
life has to offer
                    -K.S.

Windows Down

With windows down
on a breezy spring day
the sun shining
and the playlist just right
I embrace on the end of winter -
the idea that the worst is over

I like to reiterate mentally
that I've made it another day
another tough season is over
with the cold bitterness behind me
I can look ahead and find joy
in the upcoming blooms
being able to remove a layer
and still find comfort in my environment

There are very few moments
of innocent and pure peace
like listening to my favorite songs
with the windows down
listening to melodies of past loves
previous hope and previous hurt
knowing that I made it past
just able to sing along
as I keep moving forward
                    -K.S.

Kennedy Scott

New Shoes

With each time of transition
each low in life
I celebrate the ideology
that growth is possible
through anything

Like a new pair of shoes
I know I am able to go
a little further
a new beginning
without worn down soles
and the dread of old dirt

I adjust my pace
and continue walking
through my hardest days
because I am eager to embrace
the better version of me
that waits on the other side

-K.S.

Kennedy Scott

Never Be You

The only thing
that hurt more than losing you
repetitively and harshly
was realizing
if I had the chance
to do it again
I wouldn't take it

A new sense of loss
a reality I fought so hard for
isn't the reality I want
there is no happy ever after
when the history proves
uncertainty
dishonesty
and cruelty

I chose you
over and over
even at the expense
of my own well-being
but once I chose me
my own happiness
growth and prosperity
I understood
the future could never be you

-K.S.

Kennedy Scott

A Letter To Myself

As we've experienced
seasons of change
seasons of courage
seasons of love
and seasons of hope
we also had to embrace
a level of strength required
way beyond the years we grasped it

We were just a kid
we didn't deserve it
at an age we barely knew how to dress ourselves
we already knew when to hide
when to pretend to have counted sheep
so we didn't have to talk to the uniforms-
complete avoidance to acknowledge the badges
that filled our living room regularly
if we were asleep
they'd be back tomorrow with toys and stickers
to try to protect and serve the piece of innocence
we never had a shot of having

Learning survival so young
never gave us a chance to know how to live
trial and error in a pursuit of comprehension
greatness always lied in us

Kennedy Scott

Adulthood included frequently losing hope
grasping at straws
to find a reason
a grand answer to the curiosity
of the why's in life
to understand the almosts
and justify the disservice
executed not only by others
but by our own hand

A deep necessity for love
but we were capable of it all along
we didn't need external validation
we can do this ourself
we didn't have to accept the bare minimum
with a grace that justified
rewriting reality
and making it a fairytale
we no longer had to fight to survive
we deserve the chance to plant roots
and grow

Love is here
it's inside of us
it's in the glimmer of the stars
the way the sun hits the ocean
the way a new record plays
and in the way you show up for others
who wouldn't do the same for you

Kennedy Scott

Allowing growth
supersedes the pain needed to get here
we have always been more
than what was done to us
and we are worth so much more
than the attention we've passed off as love
externally sourced love is extraneous
unrequited in the quietness
of acceptance and bargaining

We've already surpassed the expectation
of milestones in the journey of life
presumed knowledge
of the unknown future
is nothing but harmful
yet understanding that the barriers
we perceive as insurmountable
are nothing more than a minor road block
we can continue to embrace
growth, love, and acceptance

I am not where I want to be but I'm on my way
                                    -K.S.

Kennedy Scott

Summer

Love, Joy, & Warmth

Nothing Better

I've been meaning to ask you
if it fits into your schedule
if we could spend the day together

I've been meaning to find out
if you've got nothing better to do
if you'd like to wake up next to each other

I've been far too nervous to ask you
I don't want to bug you
but maybe if you had the time
we could fall in love

I've been curious
if you've got some free time
and no other plans
if you could hold my hand
and call me yours
for the rest of our lives
                    -K.S.

Haven't Met You Yet

I haven't met you yet
but I feel as if you know me with a
deeper passion
sense of understanding
and comprehension
than people I've known
my whole life

I haven't met you yet
but you're the only thing I see
when I close my eyes at night
or when I imagine my future
with happiness as a possibility
in the warmest and most comfortable of times
you are what my heart longs for -
what my mind imagines
to embrace a sense of serenity

I haven't met you yet
but I feel you every day
I feel your presence
your absence
the warmth of your soul
the hope in your endeavors
and the feeling of home
in your heart

Kennedy Scott

I haven't met you yet
so I miss you with a sense of longing
I long for the hope of our paths crossing -
for coordinates to match up
and for the spark to live up
to the dream our hearts hold so dear

I haven't met you yet
but I wish for the day I finally get you
to hold in my arms
to cherish in every moment

and I fear -
even in the same room

I'll still miss you
because regardless of distance
the deepest depths of my soul longs for you
I aspire to nurture happiness and fulfillment
that allows for the happiest of days
individually and together

I haven't met you yet
but I'm counting down the days
I'll see you when we get there
and I promise with every ounce of me
I'll never look back
                    -K.S.

Kennedy Scott

Curiosity

Curiosity often breeds
unfounded imminence
electrifying intrigue
and a sense of requirement
to wonder and seek
what strikes up
such a sense of bewilderment

Nothing has struck me
quite like the curiosity
overtaking every nerve
the first time I saw you
unbeknownst to me
an overwhelming overdrive
of my inquisitive nature

I *had* to know you
who you are
what makes you smile
or what you think about
as you lay your head down

The feeling of your touch?
god it must be so soft

How it must feel to lock eyes?
the stories they must hold

Kennedy Scott

I am curious
what it could be like to be yours
even in a momentary fashion
what I wouldn't give
to have one moment

There are very few loves
that could ever equate
to the level of excitement
entrancement
and electricity
as a first moment of curiosity

As I sit here submerged
in a state of far away admiration
I can't help but wonder
if conceivably
you may be just as curious as I
we can start simply
with a conversation
and maybe someday
we'll settle on forever
                    -K.S.

Kennedy Scott

Sleep With Me

Sleep with me
as much as I do desire your touch
deep breaths
and muffled sighs
and the feeling of you on me
I mean

Fall asleep with me
let us hold one another
as we drift off into peace
let our last moment of the day
be filled with
safety
warmth
and love
allow us the vulnerability to wrap up our day
in a sense of love and togetherness

Wake up with me
let our first grasp at the morning sun
be filled with
stretches
yawns
and a yearning for that cup of coffee
but not without a desire to reach for one another
to not let go of the soul
that makes us feel so fulfilled

Kennedy Scott

Wrap me up in the comfort of you
the most vulnerable moments
authorize the greatest sense of safety
hold me and tell me I'm yours
if only for the night

Even if you let go -
if you wake up
and decide to walk away-
allow me a moment
that will live forever
a memento of a connection
I cherish every ounce of

Fall into me
allow yourself the serenity
of releasing control
fall into me and realize that
this moment together
is better than
a hundred minutes alone

Let me hold you
and assure you
everything will be okay
in this physical manifestation
of the tether our hearts hold
you'll always be with me

Kennedy Scott

Sleep with me and I won't let go
I'll be there when you wake up
and for each moment in between -
all the minutes I'd never wanna miss
I know I'll be okay
because as long as I fall asleep
I'll still be seeing you in my dreams
                                        -K.S.

Kennedy Scott

Sweet Tooth

For the first time in my life
I'm suffering from a sweet tooth
something so insatiable
that can not be satisfied
by even the sweetest treats
my craving is driven
by the sweetness of you

I am obsessed
addicted
absolutely head over heels
for the sweetness of your heart
the soft frame of your face
the richest blue in your eyes

I can not get enough of you
a hunger that will never be satisfied
I'll spend the rest of my forever
indulging in the flavor of you
embracing the sweetness of your love
always hungry for another taste
endless days with the sweetest flavor
wrapped up in each sweet nothing
the loudest whispers
telling me it's meant to be
                    -K.S.

Kennedy Scott

Tired Beauty

How lucky I feel
to see you in the moments
you don't even see yourself -
as you drift away into a night's rest
fatigue from the day
catches up to you
and as you let your guard down
and you let out the loving sentiments
you shine the brightest

The softness of your frame -
the window to the soul
I cherish with such protection
a longing
to brush my fingers across
the delicate nature
of the beauty of you

I don't dare look away
from your gentle beauty
as your soul mirrors a warrior
a strength and tenacity
to persevere and overcome
but in those intimate moments
right as you let your day rest
you've never looked more beautiful

Kennedy Scott

A strong determination
to stay true to independence
but in momentary glimpses
you allow the chance of letting someone in
creep through the cracks of defense
one day at a time
and just maybe
you'll allow yourself
to be mine

I feel so fortunate
to experience you
the beauty
the strength
the desire to not slip
but as the days go on
and I feel the butterflies come along
I know all there's left to do
is *fall*
        -K.S.

The First Time

The first time
I laid eyes on you
I was overtaken by a feeling similar to that
of the first time
I realized my future may include a *woman*
nervous
unknown
excitement

The first time
I heard your laugh
I was captivated -
overflowing with a need
much like the air in my lungs
to do anything in my power
to hear it
every
single
day

The first time
I found out
that you may like me too
it was like hearing my favorite melody
for the first time all over again
placing it on repeat
never needing to shuffle

Kennedy Scott

The first time
I looked you in your eyes
knowing the next move
was to hold you in a way I haven't before
feeling the gentle caress of your lips on mine
embracing the delicate nervousness
an awareness of the inevitable
from that first moment
I knew I didn't want a day without it

The first time
we embraced fully
with gentleness and precaution
to ensure safety and comfort
it wasn't like any *body* before
as I graced every centimeter
needing to know
what made up every bit of you
hoping someday
you'd want every bit of me

Although our first times
have gone and left
each time I lay eyes on yours
it feels new all over again
an unwavering excitement
to have a million first kisses
first glances, and first touches
spread throughout a lifetime with you

-K.S.

Kennedy Scott

Butterflies

The integrity in love
lies in the fact that at its core
it can not be falsified
the chemistry is scientific
biology kicks in
and we get the physical responses
to an emotional connection
and every time I look at you
I'm met with a swarm of butterflies

The thing about love
is it's never uncertain
and when I look at you
and I see the way you look at me
I know that what we have
is held in honesty

Between each passing glance
and lingering peer at one another
embracing the complexity
of those blue eyes
I understand
all I see is what I want for a lifetime
embracing the truth in what we could be
a future of joy and warmth
manifesting in a parcel of
butterflies

Kennedy Scott

It feels like there could be no other option
the safety and comfort
once I opened my heart to yours
felt like the soul I was meant to hold
the heart I was meant to cherish
and the future I was meant to have
it felt natural and familiar
and some people are just meant to be

I'm so glad the stars aligned
and I finally found my home
where my heart is
is wherever you are
wherever you want to go
and whoever you want to be

There is no stress in the idea of forever
lifelong love
wouldn't feel like enough
when you're the person of interest
and since timeline manifestation
does not exist beyond imagination
I'll sit and smell the roses
and simply admire
the butterflies
                    -K.S.

Waking Up

It's bordering incomprehensible -
waking up and realizing
I'd rather wake up next to you
a realization that happiness
could be a possibility
broader than my expectations could ever grasp
if I got to say you're mine

It felt like waking up when I realized
the hope of a future with you
is something my heart longs for
in a way that feels deeper than us both

Waking up has never felt so scary
the idea of wanting you chills me to my core
because wanting you opens the door
for the fear of losing you to creep in
and the reality of the possibility
that I may not get to spend the rest of my days
loving you
caring for you
and helping nurture your growth
feels like a loss I could not handle
and despite the fear -
a shot at loving you
would be of cosmic significance

Kennedy Scott

I've woken up to the feeling
of wanting to build something
grander than us both
a love so deep that a moment without it
feels like we're cheating ourselves
out of a bigger purpose

I'm awake now
with the thought of loving you on my mind
the desire to spend the days with you
a chance to find a reason
for all of the almosts in life
because without those
I never would've been able to get out of bed
and wake up
to the fact that I am falling
deeply
madly
insatiably
in love with you
                    -K.S.

Sweet Baby Blues

With luck and a gentle hope
I was able to be welcomed
with a presence so unique
where loving her for a lifetime
would be the greatest disservice
she deserves endless lifetimes
filled with the most gentle love

Looking into those sweet baby blues
I see a chance at a love overflowing
with everything I have ever wanted
embracing softness and encouraging authenticity
in the person I am and the ways I can love her
an open invitation to show up authentically -
packaged in honesty and transparency
encouragement I have never been gifted

The moment I laid my eyes on hers
and felt the warmness of her gaze
it was a level of clarity completely unmatched
any time less than an entire lifetime
and every one after this
to be able to show her safety in love
safety in trusting the hope of lifelong joy
would be dishonoring the gentleness of her heart
and the vulnerability present
in two souls intertwining

Kennedy Scott

I would spend every lifetime
ensuring the love we know as fragile
is felt and received
by the most beautifully eccentric soul
that has ever crossed my path

Every single moment
I'm able to embrace the deepest oceans
hidden within those eyes
I understand why every heartbreak has happened
so when she came around I'd know it was true
I could embrace the grand significance
and the chance for the most
honest
breathtaking
and captivating love
to drown me in the depth of the passion
almost as deep
as those sweet baby blues
                    -K.S.

7 Minutes

After our heart stops and we cease to exist
as our soul embraces the next step of moving on
our mind is left with 7 minutes
7 minutes to embrace the joys
the loves and the warmth

I'd like to believe
the reason there was no urgency
in the first move to make you mine
was a calm and collective understanding
that it was always meant to be
somewhere amidst the subconscious
I always knew you would be my home

I'd like to believe
the intensity of the realization
in the connection we were bound to share
happened with a strength and quickness
because our souls were always tied
hearts meant to interconnect
my invisible string
I was always meant to find you

I have to believe that at our cores
we understand that few loves are like this
a mutual acknowledgement
of the differences in manifestation

Kennedy Scott

Everything about *you* is different
down to the core of my being
I know there is a part of me
that is meant to fill your heart
with adoration, admiration,
and the most genuine and lighthearted obsession

I have never been more certain
that you must be my 7 minutes
the calmness intertwined
with embracing our firsts
our story was always meant to be written
we just had to find the right time
as the universe deemed fit
and the stars aligned
there is simply no better way to fill my time
than living my life
filling your heart with love
and making the memories
that will fill
those final 7 minutes

-K.S.

Kennedy Scott

Bagels and Love

Moments of care
simply symbolized
by little gestures
in our shared hours

The simple questions
making sure the other is set -
if you've eaten
or had enough water
the foundations of making oneself
healthy and happy
able to make it through the day

I see the love day in and day out
in the way your eyes shine
when they land on mine
and the way you gently ask
how you can show up for me

Through bagels and glances
glasses of water and
refrigerator light dances
I am fully aware
that this is the purest love
I have ever experienced
care is in the actions
love is in the intentions

Kennedy Scott

I do not put weight
on the hope of definitions
in a specific visualization
of a future we could hold
there is hope
but *without* expectation

With each morning bagel
I hear the whisper of
"I love you"
even without words
it's said every day

I am so excited
at the chance for a lifetime
of being woken up
by kisses on the cheek
embracing the silent moments
where the words aren't spoken
yet the sentiment is bellowed
healing parts of me
not broken by you
embracing true happiness
as not only a possibility
but a reality

*Thank you for the bagels
and thank you for loving me*
                    -K.S.

Unpacking

There's a certain patience
in loving the broken
a calmness in the approach
to try to understand
a tender reassurance alongside trying
to love *enough*
to heal the parts
you did not break

My appearance is wrapped in apologies
a constant remorse
for showing up
with remnants of bags
previously unpacked
yet you acknowledge and reassure
that although they seem impossible to carry
they are not as burdensome as they once were

Despite resurfacing
from a life previously lived
you join me just as I am
in an attempt to support and comfort
with the softest graze of my cheek
and the kindest reminder of love
you allow me to discover what was leftover
the final closure of doors left cracked

Kennedy Scott

You never hold resentment
or unnecessary predispositions
on the fact that I have believed in others
before I knew you were true
comforting me in the present
as I recognize the false nature
of each and every soul
who grazed my skin before

Your gentle approach
filled with the softest
and most serene empathy
feels undeserved
and unexpected
I don't know what to do
when I'm not met with a storm
of conflict and accusations

It's hard to be loved so wrong
yet there's still a certain difficulty
in being loved correctly
for the very first time

                    -K.S.

Ideal Love

As we grow up and grasp an ideal
of what love is supposed to be
embraced by the theory
of first looks
instant connection
invisible strings
and the concept that your soul
is magnificently designed
to embrace a specific other

If all of this is true
and that's what it's supposed to be
then I've never been more sure
that that must be the reason
you felt like home
from the very first moment

If our purpose is to love those
who are cosmically crafted for us
then the sense of belonging clicked
like the missing piece to our puzzle
knowing that your heart
was meant to dance softly with mine

You are the embodiment of an ideal love
filled with compassion and understanding
patience and gentleness

Kennedy Scott

You are each love song
every beautiful poem
and every vibrant color in the blooms
on a sunny summer day

I am so relieved I found you
and I hope we do it all again
so we find our way back home
in each and every following lifetime

-K.S.

Falling

The intrinsic bewilderment in discovery
exploration takes a hold
a patient urgency to understand
all of the little pieces
that make up
the soul that holds such a fascination

What a beautiful thing
awareness in the honesty
it feels so familiar
in the newness of it all
as if you've been around
my whole life
a familiarity in my heart knowing
a connection that was meant to be

What an absolute honor
to be aware that I'm falling
the beginning of a story
that I can't wait
to keep reading
                    -K.S.

The Clouds

I wish I could view anything
the way you view the clouds
powerful and yet gentle
an inspiring transformation
with a peaceful pace
designed for far more than just the human gaze

An inspiration battling against the monotony
in which we carry ourselves on a daily basis
paint a picture -
that is only amplified by your presence
much like the clouds
you are like a sigh of relief
after a long trial of rain

Enhance our natural strong points -
incubate the tools needed
for all of us to grow
ever giving of a selfless message
take the tools, take the rain
let it aid in your desire to flourish
and all you truly ask in return
is the joy of seeing us thrive
finally able to bloom after the drought
but not without a little help from you
a beautiful and rewarding team effort

Kennedy Scott

You are never present on conditional terms
rain, snow or shine
night or day
you are here to give us
an amplified view
of the world we see around us
the potential and the opportunity
previously hidden by a vail of
self-doubt,
self-deprecation,
and a hesitancy to ever enter the same arena that
opens up an opportunity to welcome failure
because right when we believe there is no hope
you remind us that winning
is also an option

Meeting you really was
like looking up for the first time
to see what nature has gifted us
the clouds are a reminder
that life is ever-changing
an opportunity to realize
that just because the rain is here
does not mean that we are destined to fail
because without rain there is no growth
we don't have the opportunity
to stop and smell the roses
without the cloudy days

Kennedy Scott

You are the greatest gift of all
the gift of perspective and inspiration
the gift of the ability to look inward
and see potential
a beauty even during the harshest storms

The most rewarding part
is when the rain stops
and the sun is around the bend
much like the clouds,
you remind us that even after our darkest
and heaviest times
we have the ability to open up
and let a little space in
to allow the sun to shine right through
because regardless of the weight we carried
we do not diminish in value or beauty
based on the weather of our moods
                                    -K.S.

Stargazing

I met you so long ago
always overcome with nerves
never willing to say much
fighting to find tiny morsels
of the roots of small talk
admiring from afar
never imagining
someone like *you*
could ever be intrigued
by someone like *me*

The right place
the right time
and the right push
to finally say hello
and ask you if you'd be willing
to trust and follow
have a little faith
my only way in
to our beginning

To my amazement
you took a chance
and allowed me an opportunity
to show up
and get to know you

Kennedy Scott

After giggles and nerves
I only had one question
if you're fond of the water
the nature and the stars
you looked up as you agreed
and I got lost in who you are

Constellations paint the picture
search and discovery
you looked up and got lost
yet I couldn't keep my eyes off you
and much like the night sky
the more I discover
about the person you are
the less words I have
the more entranced I am

I fall for you every single day
not letting go of the roots of us
sitting there and admiring
the beauty of you
complete astonishment
that something as perfect
as who you are
could exist at the same time
as someone as silly as me
wrapped up in the fullness of love
the gentleness of adoration
and the hope of a lifetime

Kennedy Scott

All I want
is a life of stargazing
as you embrace the night sky
holding on to the vastness
of the things much bigger than us
I can't help but keep glancing at you
every single moment
with you by my side
is far more precious
than any moment without

I know with every bit of me
that I may only get this one chance
to show you a hope and a calmness
in the risk of love
and with every bit of me
I'll spend each day
loving you with a passion
to last this lifetime and the next
in case our string gets lost
and we miss each other
in the next one

A love like this
so closely resembles each starry night
an endless adventure
still holding uncertainty
and yet providing the deepest peace
a wave of calmness
amidst the darkness of life

Kennedy Scott

I love you like I love the stars
leaving me speechless
feeling so lucky to live in a time
where we appreciate the universe
understanding the connection
the potential and the existence
the same luck I feel
when I grasp the idea
that you were made for me
and I get the opportunity
to cherish you
under a blanket of constellations
-K.S.

Kennedy Scott

Fall

Mourning, Longing, & Chasing Closure

First Choice

You were my first choice
for so long looking into my future
only seeing you
holding on to hope for us

It wasn't my first choice
to lose you
watch you walk away
remaining a subject
in small talks
amidst late nights
conversations I'm not part of

It wasn't my first choice
to let us go
but you never gave me a choice
you made the decision for us

I have to move on
but I'm a couple steps behind
still trying to understand
when that choice was made
                    -K.S.

Kennedy Scott

Idealized Perception

I miss the perspective I had
where I thought the hope between us
could carry on through anything
the idealized perception of
what we could be
and what we had
could have stood the test of time

I miss the feeling of joy
reminiscing on the times between us
before I came back to reality
and realized you were *never*
the person I thought you were

I miss little moments between us
a sense of comfort
a sense of domesticity
the peaceful days
that you presented well enough
I mistook it for love

I sometimes wonder
if you ever loved me at all
and I long for that answer
with a tenacity stronger
than the care you ever had for me

Kennedy Scott

I wish with every part of me
that there could have been truth
in the idealized perception
I had of your person
I would have given everything
for there to be integrity
in the romance I made up
fantasized on for long enough
I convinced myself it was real

I miss more than anything
the blissful ignorance I had
when it came to us
and when it came to the truth of you
you stole my heart
you took my time
and I'm left with missing someone
who
doesn't
even
exist
      -K.S.

Missing You Quietly

I will always miss you quietly
putting a guard up
so nobody has to know
I still miss you

I never know how to respond
so I always say "I'm okay"
because it's easier than saying
"I still miss her"
"I still love her"
"We should've tried"
"We could've *made* it"

I miss you quietly
so I don't look a fool
as you yell from the rooftops
that you've moved on
you're bigger and better
than what we had

I miss you quietly
so I don't have to admit
that I haven't let go
                    -K.S.

Kennedy Scott

Realized

I realized I liked you
when every notification
starting with your name
made a bad day great
and a great day
unforgettable

I realized I loved you
when you filled my soul
with a new taste of discovery
curiosity and hope
as each melody sounded brand new
all I could think of was you

I realized I *still* loved you
when even through
the coldness
of you saying goodbye
and moving on
like we never had anything
like we were never in love
I still felt warmth
when I thought of
the chance of trying again

Was it just the wrong time?
-K.S.

Kennedy Scott

Underdog

I was always the underdog
in the story of you
I was never meant
to get a chance
the first kiss
moonlight glances
midnight secrets -
nights we couldn't bear to end

But *you* gave me that chance
and right when you made me think
the underdog had won
you finally realized
if you allowed us
to write
our ever after
one day
you might have to answer
as to why you chose
the underdog

So as quickly as it began
you took control of the end
instead of a novel
we were an
unfinished sentence

Kennedy Scott

Longing for more
a cliffhanger with no answer
so I'm left with these words
and a desire to know
if things were different
and I wasn't the underdog
would you have let yourself feel
and embrace the safety of love
in the comfort of us
                    -K.S.

Quiet Truths

Late at night
when all that's left
are my solitary thoughts
and everything else is resting
the truth comes to light

In the quietest moments
when I'm most alone
with the rawest truths
and the silence of solitude
I know it's still you

The truth is so quiet
something I've buried-
a hidden observation
and an intuition
that the best chance at love
is going to be with you

We can give this a chance
we can find a forever
external perception tells me
to look elsewhere
but the quiet truths
whisper it's you
                    -K.S.

Kennedy Scott

New Number

I am constantly torn
the desire to start over
sounds so appealing
I want to get a new phone number
find a fresh start
yet I get hung up on the notion
that if I changed my number
that could be the day
you'd finally decide
you would want to say hello again
and maybe we could pick up
where we left off
                        -K.S.

Starting Over

I don't want to start over
I know you too well
my heart is far too familiar
with the gleam in your eye
and the way you express love
albeit hesitantly
it arrives in quiet abundance

I want to pick up
where we left off
to go down a different path
with an unknown outcome
exploring what alternate endings
could have looked like
in the tale of us
what we could make of them
where they could take us
a chance to write our own story

I want to love you
without the itch of past mistakes
a new endeavor
not predetermined
by nights already shared
a familiarity of my hearts home
with a refreshed sense of opportunity

Kennedy Scott

I don't want to start over
I want to keep going
I'll go wherever you want
as long as our hearts are connected
I'll weather the storms
and bathe in the sun
that is the center of you

I would love to love you
                    -K.S.

Drift Away

I will never be enough
to fit into your fairy tale
and I fear the only pieces of you I'll obtain
are the moments of fantasy
at the end of the long day

My memories play on repeat
your laughter
your smile
the way your eyes glimmer
and the passion you speak
on the things you love

if only *I* were one of them

The only remaining hope I have
to live my own happily ever after with you
live in a temporary state
in my quietest moments
I find peace
I'll drift away
and dream of you

I still love you
                    -K.S.

Kennedy Scott

I Don't Need

I don't need you to love me
I just want to know how you felt
I strive for an answer that validates
the shared connection
the shared experience
validation in mutuality

I don't need you to love me
I don't need a tomorrow
I just desire a few moments now
to understand what happened then

I don't need
definition in the what ifs
I just want to know
if I was the only one who cared

I still do
        -K.S.

Daydreaming

I frequently catch myself
in a state of daydreaming
so vividly I can still *hear* you laugh
I can still *feel* you on me
the way your touch felt against my skin
the way your lips pressed against mine
so clearly my stomach drops
as if you're right next to me

I would give anything to feel you again
to hear your nervous giggle
and catch your gaze
as you approach unknown territory
closer to me than anyone before
a trust never handed out previously
warranted only with intention
and a promise
for continued tomorrows

Skin-on-skin provided
the absence of space
much like the way you looked at me
I needed every bit of you
intertwined with every bit of me
a desire for something deeper
that far surpasses natures necessities

Kennedy Scott

I wish my daily rotation
of drifting off
into the dream
of what we could have been
would reflect in reality
and I would have the chance
to hear you say my name again
through late night muffled secrets

does it still count as daydreaming
if it happens the most
at night
          -K.S.

Prosperity

We connected
in a state of spontaneity
and you left just as unexpectedly

You said
it was for your own prosperity
I can't help but wonder
how you thought
I would hinder that
when all I was offering
was love
       -K.S.

Home

Please know
for as long as my heart beats
you will have a home
a place to lay down your worries
take the stress off your plate
and let yourself unwind

Regardless of how long we may be apart
please know
your home will be waiting for you
just as you left it
ready to continue our story
but with fresh flowers
on your bedside table
and a stronger will
to never let go
                -K.S.

Status

It was never a point of status-
the desire to love you
never came from a place
of wanting to show off

Rooted in the desire
to know you
to love you
and see you
in a way you haven't before

Safety is uncomfortable
it takes a leap of faith
to fall in love
to find stability and comfort
in the dynamics that start
with violent *dis*comfort

It wasn't a status afterwards
as we shared silent moments
veiled by silence and secrecy
not something to brag on
not something to speak on
I wanted to love you for no one but us
I still could love you
-K.S.

Kennedy Scott

No Amount of Poetry

No amount of poetry
no string of words
nor beauty in perspective
could honor how badly
I want you back home with me

-K.S.

Kennedy Scott

Still

I still get the urge to reach out
text you
raise the white flag
for a war I did not start

I still hope
one day you might come around
and realize the authenticity in us
and I'll get a chance
to show you I wasn't lying
when I said I'd wait for you

Despite the hurt
I'd still choose you
　　　　　　　　-K.S.

Kennedy Scott

The Last

Life is a collection
of firsts and lasts
awareness hugs the firsts
embracing new beginnings
the hope and the beams of light
but so many lasts
lie in secrecy

The last time
I looked in your eyes
I believed with every ounce of me
our glances would meet again

The last time
I said goodbye
I thought it was for the night
I didn't know
it would be forever

The last time I held you
under the impression
that our embrace
would always find a way back home
I never could have imagined
the second I let go
you'd find somebody else

Kennedy Scott

I never would have imagined
the last time I saw you
would be the last time
I *ever* saw you
I always thought
I'd get another call
letting me know
you were ready to see me again

I mourn so many of my lasts
wishing I could have known
they were finales
and the most heartbreaking bit
is knowing much like our lasts
maybe I didn't hold on
tightly enough
to all of our firsts

-K.S.

Kennedy Scott

Winter

Grief, Sadness, Bitterness & Anger

Too Good To Be True

I feel trapped
in the ever sinking hole
convincing myself
that happiness is simply
too good to be true

Every time I get close
to being able to hold on
when I allow myself the hope
of accepting joy
safety and love
it gets flipped
and I get left behind

It feels too good to be true
because it always has been

I want to find peace in happiness
-K.S.

Kennedy Scott

Unnecessary Villains

Reaching a point
of acceptance
reaching a point
of ignorance-
understanding-
no matter how hard I try
for a select few
there has to be a villain

Without the awareness
to look within
you can only look outwards
point a finger
pull the trigger
you've taken your aim
and I'm taking the blame

A lesson to be learned -
but an enemy isn't required
love isn't a conflict
no need for a war
to bury a love
most would die for
without a honorable end
we fall victim to
a falsified battle

Kennedy Scott

You felt the need
to vilify me
as if to search for a justification
a reason you had to leave
but the truth was enough -
timing doesn't match

I just wish
you could've left
and found a way
to accept the reality of peace
in your attempt to process
that you chose to lose me

-K.S.

You Didn't Mean It

You tell me you didn't mean it
unlike each embrace we shared
when you swore it was genuine
rooted in honesty and value
assuring me I had nothing to worry about
that you would still be around
regardless of what happened

You tell me you didn't mean it
but how would you have known
that the decisions you made
would make me question everything
a complete dismantling
of the trust I fought so hard
to hold in others
to allow myself to have faith
that maybe people could
be good, hold integrity or value
even after things end
in the person I am
and how hard I tried

You didn't mean it
yet that doesn't change the outcome
but I guess that's on me
because I'm the one who believed you

Kennedy Scott

You told me you didn't mean it
but how am I to trust such a sentiment
how am I to believe the intentions
when the same mouth
that told me the hurt wasn't intentional
also told me
that our time meant something
and yet you left so easily

*You weren't honest then
and you aren't honest now*
                    -KS

Turnaround

It's breathtaking how quickly
a turnaround can occur
something so special yesterday
is something you cover up today

You haven't moved on
and neither have I
we're showing it differently -
I hide in silence while you express so loudly
desperate to find fault
in a connection with none

How can I be *everything* one day
and *nothing* the next
was I just a hometown secret?
something you couldn't bear to face
amidst your facade of reality
or was the reality of us too genuine to hold
in the dishonesty of your persona

I was good enough in secret
yet something so easily denied
nobody was asking - except yourself
in response to self-reflection
was it real?
you just weren't ready for it

Kennedy Scott

A string of secrets
special moments under moonlight
nobody knew
and when it came to an end
it stayed with us
until the yearning for a reason
led to making it passively publicized
running after an answer
amidst the unknown

I didn't need an answer
I just wanted you
void of ill-will
we can still make peace
                    -K.S.

Kennedy Scott

Questions

It's not that you made me question
my worth
or if I'm desirable
I don't need any help
putting those in question
it's the fact
that you made me question
entire foundations
of who I call a friend
because after you made it platonic
you turned around to twist the knife
and thought I would never find out

I don't need any assistance
in questioning myself
I'm always on a mission
to prove I'm enough
an overcompensation for an arena of doubt
that overshadows any compliment
or ribbon of hope
because I always justify
a misread connection
or a difference in views
as an inherent flaw in my ability to love
or the way I look
there must be something wrong
I must be the problem

Kennedy Scott

I have a hard enough time
proving my worth to myself
trying to add value to the monotony of existing
faking it and hoping I can make it
because it is hard enough to battle my own head
without others putting my character
into question
but you take your stage and ignore the pain

I question every single day
if one day I'll be enough
not in a way where I seek validation-
rather an honest evaluation
of whether or not I can find a voice
amidst the darkness
to show up with a firmness and an acceptance
that is deep enough
to not have to question
if the reason you hurt others
is somehow my fault

That's on me
                    -K.S.

A Little Getaway

It must be such a relief
to be able to leave consequences behind
all you have to do
is commit the hurt
and walk away
for a little getaway

Like a vacation
after battling the long days
but contrary to a 9-5
the pain you inflicted never closed
and as you left me to deal
with the aftermath of you -
your broken promises
your lack of integrity
and your inability
to take accountability

I wish I was able
to get away
from the downfall of you
the anxiety of the
impending outcome
that you'll reach out
right as I'm getting over you

Kennedy Scott

You don't hold that space anymore
because someone who can
hurt others so carelessly -
putting more effort into acting
like it never happened
than you do
owning up to your actions
is not someone I want
to reserve space for
                    -K.S.

Empty

It's funny to me how heavy
feeling empty can be
the burden of disconnection
the weight of dissociating
not a drop of thought
just making it through until it overwhelms
and I let a few tears out to relieve the pressure

I know you're happier and that's good-
that your own actions don't carry the weight
on your shoulders as they do on mine
the effect of your decisions weighs me down
with a strength and a heaviness
I can not stand to bear

The downfall of your actions
disrupt more than just the people
you keep in arms reach
a ripple effect of hurt
a continuation of pain

It's not all you -
it's my inability to comprehend
to understand the acceptance
and the willpower to hurt others
and look past the impact it has

Kennedy Scott

I almost admire your willingness
to leave things in the moment -
to hurt and let it go
leave it behind
to let others pick up the pieces
of your destruction

I'm lost in the empty
the heaviness of the feeling
and the lack thereof
I'm dealing with what *you* left behind-
a collection of the remnants
of the presence you had
before you ran away
and claimed
that the ignorance of your destruction
is justified
in the name of
self-improvement
self-growth
and the pursuit of strength

I'm stuck with the emptiness
trying to find the pieces of me again
to feel anything at all
after the emptiness of your person

-K.S.

Kennedy Scott

The Sweetest Revenge

The sweetest revenge
is knowing I have control
over certain people
only getting access
to specific versions of me

The sweetest revenge
comes from growth
and leaving those who are
stagnant
self-absorbed
and stuck
in a string of half-truths
behind

you'll never know this version of me
-K.S.

Kennedy Scott

The Difference Between You and I

There are many identifiers
between individuals -
differences that both
bring us together
and keep us apart
something to be celebrated
something to be valued

I make the decision
to celebrate the beauty
and memorialize the individuality
in a way to honor and protect
something I used to hold dear
because doing otherwise
would be dishonest

You choose to create a narrative
an idea of me that's anything but
picture perfect
flattering
or honest
in a way to protect yourself
from the difficulty of having to try
to look inwards
and face the parts of yourself
that require a little maintenance

Kennedy Scott

The difference between you and I
is a sense to get better
a level of integrity
that allows us to evolve
in a way that is beyond
what we do
to get out of bed
every single day

Integrity goes beyond
the words we say
integrity lies in our
character and the
ways in which we
decide to respond to
situations that challenge
our perception of ourselves

Although you never stop
looking in the mirror
or viewing yourself
through a camera lens
you lack a real ability
to reflect on anything
beyond the way your makeup lies
beauty is only skin-deep
to someone who constantly avoids
facing what's on the inside

Kennedy Scott

The difference between you and I
is I value the opportunity to reflect
and pick apart the pieces of me
that make me less
than my full potential

The difference between you and I
is I value my own character
more than I value outside perception
because I am more than
what is said about me
and I am more
than what you tried
to make me out to be
                    -K.S.

Kennedy Scott

My Last Good Day

Sometimes
I wonder if I've had my last good day
if the darkness
that clouds the sun
is the rest of what I'll see

I often ponder
if looking into your eyes
was the last time
I'll ever feel
the hope of love
maybe that's why it hurt so much -
the day you walked away
because I can't help but wonder
if that was my last chance

I often ask myself
when I'll have
my last good day
will I know?
will it be with intention?
or just an accident?
the light before
I proceed through the tunnel
with no end in sight

Kennedy Scott

I always hope
that when I have
my last good day
I'm able to soak it in
appreciate it for what it is
a romance intertwined with life
a chance to enjoy the sweet moments
in this world that can be so bitter

I look forward to the possibility
of still having my last good day
that this heavy burden
this expansive darkness
isn't what will fill
the rest of my days
                    -K.S.

Quicksand

When the days start
to feel a little darker
and I catch myself slipping
it often feels like quicksand
unable to save myself
and yet the more I fight
the quicker I sink

It drags me under
with an unparalleled vigor
an all encompassing expanse
of a vast darkness
hopelessness
and desperation-
a fight for my life
to find a sense of light again

A battle unlike any other
the deepest need
to find the lining of hope once more
looking for silver
only to find the void of color
an absence of encouragement
excitement
and personality
matched with an eagerness
to find a reason to keep moving forward

Kennedy Scott

I battle to get out
and once I get there
it's a never-ending war to never fall back
yet right as I let my guard down
and I embrace the hope
that safety could become a norm
I start sinking once again
wondering why the days
start to feel lower
and not until it's far too late
to simply take a step out
do I realize I'm up to my neck

I want the opportunity
to live my days
without the fear of quicksand
for now I'll make it through
another cloudy day
in anticipation
that someday
I may not have to fear
the quickness of sinking
                    -K.S.

Kennedy Scott

Silent Love

I've become aware of the position in my life
knowing that I've accepted normalcy
in being loved so quietly
hidden behind the walls of secrecy
the idea of being known
let alone celebrated
is so foreign

Accepting a one-sided quiet love
leaves space for missed connections
assumption in intentions
and misunderstood conversations

The concept of being a part
of the story I help write
held in a place where I am recognized
for the heart I have
the love I give
and the effort I exude
is as foreign as success in a forever

Being loved with volume
is a dream I haven't grasped
something not yet
discovered beyond imagination
a theory not yet seen in practice
imagery in being left speechless

Kennedy Scott

Love has always been limited
to private listening sessions
settling for lukewarm celebrations
of melodies half finished
with a little doctoring
they have been repackaged
as lyrical wonders
to stand the test of time
when we were never meant to be more
than a one-hit wonder

I want to be loved in stereo
to have it as the background
amongst holidays with friends
family and loved ones

I want to be more than a silent love
                              -K.S.

Evolving Truths

I look back at our time together
understanding how our truth evolved
knowing there was a day
I tried to convince myself
you were the only love for me
realizing that I was more in love
with the way I loved you
and the potential to give that to the right person
than I was with *us*

True love can not flourish
in one-sided connections
it's detrimental enough
to feel a lack of appreciation
but it's even more heartbreaking
to have the way I show up
feel like a burden
an inconvenience in your pursuit of joy
when the whole time I thought
I was a part of it

I pursued love blindly
to the fact that I was trying so hard
to convince myself I was capable of it -
loving fully and authentically
in a manner that would justify someone staying

Kennedy Scott

I can not find lifelong adoration
if I'm only focused on what I can give
love is a two-way road
I need it as much as I need to give it
but I was left in a roundabout of settling
and once I proved my point that *I* could love
I realized I needed the other half

I wasn't dishonest when I said
you were the love of my life
it did not come from a place of disingenuity
but reality changes the dynamics of truth
an ever-changing understanding
led to comprehension
that you would never be able
to love me in a way
that could last more than a few months
let alone a lifetime

Our truth evolved
once I realized
you were *not* the love of my life
rather I am completely infatuated
with the idea of someone loving me
as much as I have tried to love others

-K.S.

Kennedy Scott

Sinking Ships

With each beginning voyage
there's a risk we take
at the most simplified level
it's success vs. failure
sinking or sailing

We were meant to make it
our friendship was supposed to last
beyond the what if's and could be's
you assured me I could trust
as an integral part of my daily
as an integral part of your healing

Once I didn't depend on you
and had multiple sources of joy
happiness and love
you steered us far off course
and our ship instantly sank

I didn't even get a chance
to process we were going down
before I was underwater
fighting for one last breath
a desire to understand
why I was drowning
wondering where you went
when you said you'd stick around

Kennedy Scott

Unconditional
is supposed to mean
through *any*thing
and I never would have bet
that my happiness
and a new source of love
would be the deal breaker

I mourn our voyage
but even more so
I wish you had meant what you said
when you said presence
would be everlasting
through the harshest storms
and the brightest days

You helped me process
previous delays in sailing the seas
endings of dynamics
and previously sunken ships
I just never thought
we would be one of them

-K.S.

Kennedy Scott

Too Late

It fills me to the brim
with ire and resentment
that just as I predicted
the moment I moved on
you came around

You were far too late
realizing I was the one
knowing what we could have been
and where we could have gone

I now understand
that it wouldn't have worked
regardless of if we *had* tried
you were never meant for me

You were too late
to honor the connection we started with
I am *not* the one who got away
I am the one you *gave* away
now *you* have to sit with that
the outcome would not have changed
we would've gone down different paths
but how dare you
claim to be
better than my own happiness
how dare you play the victim

Kennedy Scott

The only victimhood
is by your own hand
and someday
maybe
hopefully
you'll realize
that you *do* have power
in the cards life deals you

I don't wish you ill
I don't wish you misfortune
but I do wish you wake up
and you don't miss another love like mine
before it's too late
                    -K.S.

Polaroids

Nothing hurt
quite like cleaning in spring
finding old remnants of you
polaroids and bracelets
tucked away and faded
just like the memories of us

You gave me a hope
wrapped up in fresh sobriety
that life would move on
without desertion in dissociation
but that hope was just a snapshot
an empty exemplification
of imagery so easily lost
just like the photos of us
on that cold winter night

                    -K.S.

Kennedy Scott

Hopeful Desperation

I am overflowing
with the feeling of hope
but with a sense of mournful urgency
I hope so badly that I'm right
about you
about us
about what our future can hold

I am so tired of being wrong
ignoring my gut and finding a way
to market false promises
as everlasting love
but with you even my gut agrees

I want it to be you
with every bit of me
I want a sense of the dream
the white picket fence
a fairytale ending that lasts a lifetime

I want to be the one
to show you a lifetime of love
and with an overwhelming sense
of desperation in hope
I want to be right about you
I *need* to be right about you

Kennedy Scott

You gave me a chance
and every fiber of my being
is filled to the brim with fear
that you'll change your mind
and decide to give a different love a try

My love may not be perfect
I have always been the underdog
but I can promise you
it will last forever
just stick with me
please
we can make it

I don't have faith
that I can handle another loss
and you are far different than the rest
every love has led to you
and if I ever lost you
I don't know what I'd do

Just once I want to be enough
I want to be somebody's everything
I look at you and see a lifetime
all I can do is hope
that you see me and think the same
in this whirlwind
of hopeful desperation
                    -K.S.

Kennedy Scott